Be Strategic:

Create a Healthy Organization

Wendy L. Kuhn

Copyright © 2017 Wendy Leigh Kuhn

All rights reserved.

ISBN: 1542595479
ISBN-13: 978-1542595476

DEDICATION

To my parents who always, always taught me to follow my dreams and to my husband who helps to make them come true.

CONTENTS

Contents

Introduction 1
Chapter 1: The Research Says - Build a Healthy Organization 3
Chapter 2: Strategic Planning 7
Chapter 3: Implement Microbursts to Revitalize your Strategic Plan..... 17
Chapter 4: You've Committed to Change, Now What? 25
Chapter 5: Healthy Project Management 29
Chapter 6: Healthy Communications 37
Chapter 7: Resilience at Work 51
Chapter 8: Be Happy at Work 61
Chapter 9: Continue at Home 75
Chapter 10: What's Next? 85

Introduction

After working in government, non-profit, and corporate America, I decided it was time to take some time off. My husband and I spent half a year traveling and a lot of time thinking. I realized a number of things, not the least of which was that after working for two impossible bosses, I no longer wanted someone else to control my time and direction. Working for myself was my dream that through hard work and perseverance became a reality.

Having faced down breast cancer once, I also knew that I did not want to go through that particular experience again and that I wanted to do whatever I could to help others to avoid it. To that end, I became a holistic health coach and a HeartMath® mentor

As my journey continued, I began to think about the intersection between the work one-on-one work that I was doing with clients and the strategic planning and implementation work I was doing for businesses, non-profit, and governments.

It became increasingly clear to me that the lack of attention to employee wellbeing in the workplace is a huge contributor to stress and poor health and to failed projects, decreased bottom lines, and lack of satisfaction at work.

While researching how the question of wellness in the workplace is being addressed in many organizations, I realized that the separation between wellness programs and the operations of an organization often meant that benefits were left on the table and employees and employers were not reaping the rewards of a healthy work force.

Simultaneously, yet another article in the local paper about why projects fail led me to research data on project failures. While the numbers of failures (or not living up to expectations) are astonishing and hugely impactful, this was not the most surprising element to me. More surprising and troubling was that the reasons offered for why projects fail were that they same lessons learned I had toiled over twenty years earlier. It felt like we were not learning anything. And, then, I had my "aha" moment. Perhaps, it was that we were identifying and learning the wrong lessons. That, in fact, project failures were at least partially fueled by inattention to the wellbeing of employees and, even more so, doing things that specifically harmed employees.

While incorporating these findings into my work, and offering talks on these topics, my husband became fascinated with how the brain works. We quickly realized the huge overlap in the work that we were both doing. The brain functions better when we pay attention to our wellbeing as we can now measure through fMRIs. It turns out, for example, we do need sleep, that walking can increase our creativity, and that feeling gratitude can lead to better outcomes.

As I continue this journey, I have compiled my articles, research, blogs, and newsletters into the following book. It can be read cover to cover or pick a topic of interest and go straight there.

May it be of service to you.

Chapter 1: The Research Says - Build a Healthy Organization

When I was in high school, college and even graduate school, if we had a gnarly research question to figure out, we went to the library and spent hours poring through old journals, books, microfiche, and card catalogs. In many ways, finding sources that could be trusted was easier than today, but access to information overall is leaps and bounds beyond what it used to be. I still get excited every time someone comes up with a question or I am in the midst of a debate and I'm able to look up the answer and give a quick response. Just last week I was able to find out how old Joni Mitchell is (and that she seemed to be doing well after being rushed to the emergency room) and find the quickest route to my destination – in moments!

A few facts that guide the work that I do:

Project and strategic plan failure is costly and adoption of organizational change is an important component

- According to Gallup, "One estimate of IT failure rates is between 5% and 15%, which represents a loss of $50 billion to $150 billion per year in the United States. Another study estimated that IT project failures cost the European Union €142 billion in 2004."

- Also according to the Gallup Healthways study, employees who feel their managers are concerned about their wellbeing perform better - Employees who say they have more supportive supervisors are 1.3 times as likely to stay with the organization and are 67 percent more engaged.

Wasted meetings are costly even before looking at the costs of poorly made or implemented decisions as the result of ineffective meetings

- According to a study[1] cited by Fuze.com, the estimated annual cost of wasted meetings globally is $37 billion.

We are an unhealthy nation and this is costly to the bottom line

- According to the Milliken Institute, in 2003 the productivity losses associated with the seven chronic diseases of cancer, mental disorders, diabetes, heart disease, hypertension, pulmonary conditions, and stroke totaled almost $1.1 trillion, while treatment expenditures totaled $277.0 billion. Together, the combined economic impact of these diseases amounted to $1.3 trillion and more than half of all Americans suffer from one or more chronic disease. A study by Loeppke and colleagues in the Journal of Occupational and Environmental Medicine finds that the costs of productivity loss were four

---

[1] https://digest.bps.org.uk/2013/03/20/the-scourge-of-meeting-late-comers/

times as great as the direct medical costs of a chronic condition.

- According to the Task Force on Rural Health, North Carolina is the 16th most overweight/obese state in the nation.

Health and wellness programs are costly and often underutilized

- According to the Rand Corporation, corporate wellness is a $6 billion industry. yet according to Gallup Healthways only 24% of employees who have a wellness program use.

By integrating these efforts – the running of the business and the health and wellness of employees, we can attain positive results. Here are some important points to consider:

Healthier employees are more productive and save the company money through:

- Decreased corporate medical costs (for self-insured organizations)
- Decreased absenteeism and presenteeism (when people are present but not productive)
- Increased morale
- Increased retention.

Healthy Approaches improve outcomes, for example:

- Walking improves creativity.
- Exercise is good for your brain as well as your body.
- Stretching can cause the brain to think about problems more creatively.
- Eating healthier and breathing fresh air increase energy.
- Getting adequate sleep improves mood and performance.

Chapter 2: Strategic Planning

A brand new strategic planning project with a client is exciting. The possibilities are endless and creative ideas abound with almost everything "on the table."

As the project progresses, reality often sets in. There are political considerations and cost considerations; under pressure, business relationships are tested; operations can interfere with brainstorming or production time; and life, sometimes interferes. This is when it gets most interesting. It becomes possible to understand what can really happen and what must fall off for now. Watching an organization begin to adopt change and figure out how to be successful in a new dynamic is exhilarating and motivating. The opportunity to be a part of creating the vision, facilitating that change, and seeing an organization achieve success based on the plan is intensely satisfying.

When I approach a new strategic planning project, it is often like a puzzle. I am not a fan of a one size fits all approach, rather I take my experience, my knowledge of best practices, and the specific elements that I learn about the organization and work closely with them to co-create an approach that will work for them When the approach works, we will usually develop a plan that also works for them. Here are some of the key tenets of my approach.

Substance

It is often tempting to create a beautifully worded plan, with mission and vision statements that ultimately do not say anything. On some level it can be richly rewarding to have a group of people nod in agreement at the end of a long day of a facilitated session and state "we will make the world a better place," or "our widgets will be the best widgets," or "apple pie is delicious." Without a substantive plan to support this, a specific approach that makes this organization's strategy more likely to be effective than someone else's, and a shared understanding of what the words mean, it is unlikely to be a successful plan.

In developing clear specific guidelines for a future looking organization, it is an art to recognize that in today's changing world the specific or target might change. And that is an art, well worth the time to develop. A plan with a vision of the intended future state is a powerful way to guide and direct an organization. Even better is plan that is a "living" document that can be updated within the spirit of the plan as the organization evolves and the environment changes.

Priorities

It is also tempting, especially when good, substantive ideas are surfacing and energizing everyone, to include all of the ideas in the plan. While it's great to create a big list to work from and create

energy and enthusiasm, without priorities, the strategic plan is difficult if not impossible to implement. People feel they can pick and choose which ones to work on and scattered resources get frustrated with incremental if any progress. Budget arguments often flare and controversy ensues without clear resolution.
Often initiatives find themselves in direct conflict with each other.

By establishing strategic priorities through a collaborative approach, the organization is able to move forward with purpose and direction. Because the priorities have been jointly agreed, there are fewer organizational squabbles over limited resources.

Buy In

Even the most substantive, well prioritized, well written strategic plan will fall apart without buy in from staff, management, customers, Board members and other stakeholders. It is tempting to wait to share information until the plan is fully birthed; it feels less confusing and more exciting and inspired. Staff who are used to leaders who come and go, who feel that their livelihood is tied to the way they have always done things, who believe that strategic planning is code for layoffs, or who feel rebuffed by or removed from the process can sink a plan far more quickly than a significant change in the marketplace or some other external factor.

With buy in, staff are committed to rowing in the same direction as their leaders. They are often newly re-energized and re-focused. Ideally, they see "what's in it for me" in the plan. When this happens, a plan's likelihood of success is geometrically increased.

To achieve a substantive, prioritized strategic plan with appropriate buy in across all stakeholders, there are some key pieces to include.

Learn from the past

Especially when a new senior team comes in, or a new consultant, it is easy to take the path of rejecting the old in favor of the new. Often there is much in the old that can be rejected and there are nuggets in the old that are priceless. A practice or process that seems dated and useless may be based on something very practical that may or not be able to be changed, but that definitely requires attention Getting to the core reasons for a process or approach will take skillful facilitation.

Pay attention to best practices, the marketplace, trends, and the competition

While every organization is different, it is also the case that there is no need to reinvent the wheel every single time. It is not necessary to take what has been said or done before as set in stone, but it is likely that there will be valuable lessons as well as cautionary tales that are worth paying attention to. Moreover, in engaging in conversations and research about best practices, the marketplace and the general state of the industry will yield benefits for the strategic plan and may create valuable partnerships and relationships that will add value in the future.

Collaborate

It's tempting to believe that we can do this alone, after all isn't a camel a horse designed by a committee? Our ideas are interesting, as the new CEO of an organization or an external consultant, we were likely hired, at least in part because of our ideas, our commitment to shake up the status quo, and to bring in a breath of fresh air.

Yet, in today's complex world there is increasingly evidence, not just in strategic planning but in organizational management that collaboration is key. It is not possible to have access to or understand all of the information that is available and the rapid pace of change makes it critical that collaboration be a key part of any strategic planning effort, otherwise the document will become irrelevant before it is even completed.

There is a great scene in the movie "Hidden Figures" where the lead character insists on attending the daily briefing because otherwise by the time she can generate the numbers needed for the space launch, they would already be obsolete. By her participation in the meeting and the other participants willingness to collaborate with her, albeit begrudgingly, she, and they, achieved success.

Incorporate Healthy Practices (into the planning process and the Plan)

To create an excellent strategic plan, participants need to be fully engaged in what is often a long and sometimes tedious process. Healthy practices throughout the process will result in more engaged participants and a more successful strategic plan. This can occur in a number of ways

- Conduct healthy meetings. Serve water and healthy snacks, take frequent breaks, manage to a clearly defined agenda and set of goals, and engage in exercises that stimulate creativity.

- Set realistic expectations. Recognize that people are probably fully employed in the ongoing operations of their organization (whether it is internal or external). Work with them to develop a strategy that enables them to fully participate in the strategic planning effort without putting at risk their ability to do their jobs and get a good nights' sleep.

Incorporating employee wellness into the fabric of a strategic plan is key to demonstrating to employees that their wellbeing is valued by the organization, achieving improved bottom line results for the organization, and increasing the likelihood of the strategic plan being successfully adopted.

Strategies to do this could include:

- A pillar in the strategic plan expressing a commitment to employee wellbeing with the ability to budget projects to support this pillar. For example, a budget to support team volunteer activities, participation in a 5K, a walking trail, or a cafeteria with healthy options.
- Within specific priorities or goals a recognition of the need for paying attention to employee wellbeing. For example, if a strategic goal is to create a world class customer support center, the Plan should include a description of how the employees' wellbeing will be supported.
- If a strategic goal is to increase productivity of the organization, it should include a description of how an element of this will be ensuring employees have adequate ability to access healthy food, exercise, community activities, etc.

Be Inclusive (of staff and the community)

It is tempting in developing a strategic plan to just work with those who seem most interested and motivated by it or to ignore current customers in the quest for new customers. Travel to places where your customers or employees are. Talk to people in a facilitated session, in a small group or individually, or over a meal. Learn what they think; recognize the value in what they say. These very conversations may lead to a decision to change the role of a staff person or to change a line of business, but first have the conversations.

Co-create

As a consultant, it is tempting to gather all of the information and then go hide out in a home office and type up a strategic plan; turn it into the client, send a bill, and move on. This will not produce the best outcome.

In co-creating a strategic plan with a client, you open them up to the possibilities of what can be done and allow them the ability to extend the co-creation to their team and their stakeholders. While this will lead to drafts flying around and word choices argued over, *at the end, it results in a better plan and one that is embraced by the organization and the community.*

Communicate

I am always astounded at how easy it is to under communicate given the vast array of choices available for communications and the number of tweets, emails, phone messages, and meetings that occur over, well, absolutely everything. Communication about a strategic plan is critical. It is about making sure the appropriate information is available to the right people at the right time. This can be tricky. Over communicate too early and you may be sharing an approach that is infeasible or will quickly be canned. Communicate too late and people feel undervalued and ignored. Hit the sweet spot and the implementation of the strategic plan will flow smoothly.

As a result...

Not only will this approach result in a stronger, better, more implementable strategic plan, but it will also pave the way for organizational change. Without staff, community, and management willingness to implement changes, strategic plans turn into pretty documents sitting on the shelf.

To create a plan that will be implemented and tracked, it must be one where people recognize that they have a voice and a contribution and that they are valued.

Wendy Kuhn

Chapter 3: Implement Microbursts to Revitalize your Strategic Plan

Developing a strategic plan can be tricky. Implementing it and staying consistent with it are far more challenging. I find that:

- Employees and others are not often familiar with the mission and vision statement let alone the details of a strategic plan.
- Staff do not know the components of the strategic plan or have a sense that what they do furthers the strategic direction of the organization.
- Organizations miss opportunities because they are wedded to a strategic direction that has become outdated or irrelevant.
- Words that are uttered in passing become enshrined as gospel in the strategic plan.

I recently conducted a facilitated session for an organization and asked them what was in their mission statement. None of the people present, mostly Board members, could answer. The reason this surprised me is that the mission statement was written on a flip chart sheet clearly visible to all of them.

All too often when I talk to people about their strategic plans, they do not know any of the elements or they can recite the words but don't know (or possibly care) what they mean or how they apply to the organization.

I am a big believer in the value of consensus, the power of the collective, and the benefits of facilitated sessions that reach out to employees, customers, and other stakeholders for strategic planning efforts. At the same time, I am aware that, all too often, words from these sessions can be twisted, misunderstood or become dogma. Something said casually can easily become set in stone. A quick aside, a summary from tired participants, or a flawed voting or prioritization process can mean that the direction set for the organization is created without intent or deliberate choice. This is a disadvantage to the organization and is unfair to those who devote their time and effort to making an organization more effective.

Frequently, strategic plan goals seem to be lofty or unachievable. For some, it is hard to tie day-to-day operations to the strategic plan. This can be disheartening and un-empowering for employees toiling for an employer who they believe fails to recognize the value of their efforts. Additionally, these goals can be become irrelevant or outpaced by the marketplace or technology and linger long after they are meaningful or helpful.

There are notable exceptions and these exceptions tend to be highly successful businesses. They also tend to have employee wellbeing as a key component of the strategic plan.

In the Human Performance Institute's White Paper, "The Power of an Energy Microburst,"[2] Janet Nikolovski, Ph.D. and Jack Groppel, Ph.D. talk about the fact that work is a series of sprints with times for recovery in between, not a marathon. In fact, it is often during the recovery that we have the best ideas. They define a microburst as "*a small (short in duration), intentional activity that results in a disproportionate, higher return.*"

This applies to strategic planning as well. Rather than looking at it as a marathon over several years, think of breaking it into sprint like pieces with microbursts along the way. Moreover, with the advent of 24x7 information cycles and access and the expectation of instantaneous responses, we often "micro-learn" enough for the next step or to move forward slightly, before acquiring the next piece of information. It is a very different model than many of us grew up with before access to information was so quick and response times so short.

Strategic planning microbursts are a great way to make significant forward progress on a strategic plan, increase its visibility, and build excitement and energy for its successful completion. Engaging everyone or a business unit in a microburst is a great way to demonstrate the relevance and accessibility of the strategic plan even while setting powerful, far reaching targets.

---

[2]https://www.researchgate.net/publication/258867461_The_Power_of_an_Energy_Microburst

Microbursts are consistent with exercise approaches (think interval training), e-learning, recommended work techniques (such as Pomodoro), IT development (think Agile and Scrum), and 21st century attention spans. Embracing this approach offers an opportunity to revitalize your organization and your strategic plan, thereby increasing your relevance.

Implementing strategic plan microbursts in your organization is a great way to:

- Increase the relevance of your strategic plan
- Increase awareness of the strategic plan
- Ensure that it maintains currency and vitality
- Enhance its resilience
- Demonstrate organizational commitment to the tenets, principles, and initiatives embodied in the plan.

Employing principles of wellbeing as part of the strategic planning microburst will:

- Increase acceptance of the plan
- Demonstrate organizational commitment to employees
- Increase loyalty and productivity
- Create better outcomes
- Improve the bottom line.

A strategic plan microburst is a period of intense, defined effort on a specific element or elements the strategic plan. It is designed to achieve progress, increase awareness, and generate enthusiasm for the direction of the organization.

- The strategic plan itself could incorporate this process or it can be developed after the fact.
- It can involve the entire organization or an organizational unit.
- It recognizes the importance of employee wellbeing – employees are not expected to do their "day jobs" and then also participate in a microburst AND it incorporates employee wellbeing as a part of the effort.
- It makes specific, tangible progress towards achieving a defined strategic plan objective.
- It is within the context of a governance program that ensures consistency of purpose across the organization, appropriate prioritization, and effective communication.

To micro-burst your strategic plan, in a healthy manner that is mindful of employee wellbeing, make sure you do the following:

- **Start with a plan.** Create a solid strategic plan with employee engagement and consideration for employee wellbeing.

- **Maintain currency.** Create a focus group or alternative approach to test key elements or assumptions of the strategic plan. If something is outdated or irrelevant, consider adjusting it rather than waiting for the next refresh cycle.

- **Involve employees in the design.** Solicit employee involvement in the design of the microburst and its subsequent evaluation.

- **Communicate.** Announce the microburst along with the specific targets associated with it and communicate throughout the process.

- **Measure.** Identify specific, measurable targets.

- **Improve employee wellbeing.** As part of the microburst, identify at least one specific element focused on employee wellbeing. Examples include:
    - Creating a team to participate in a volunteer activity or a 5K.
    - Including stress management training as part of a systems implementation.
    - Providing a trail for walking, running, or other exercise as part of an office move.
    - Upgrading to a healthier cafeteria as part of a new product launch.

- **Tell your story.** Document successes.

- **Move on.** Take the success and then move forward.

- **Remember it's a microburst.** Take appropriate breaks in between microbursts.

- **Set realistic expectations.**
  If employees are working on a microburst, recognize that other efforts might fall behind. Be clear on priorities and expectations.

Microbursts provide an opportunity for currency and relevance of the strategic plan to be an integral part of an organization's operations while also making specific, measurable progress towards important goals.

Wendy Kuhn

Chapter 4: You've Committed to Change, Now What?

co-written with Pamela Erskine[3]

Are you ever bewildered by how challenging it can be to implement changes in your organization? Are you seeking to achieve buy in and support for your initiatives and day-to-day operational changes? Several methodologies exist, but they overlook a crucial principle – to support your organization, your employees need to feel supported by the organization. They need to feel that the company and their leadership care about them and their wellbeing. Consider how a health and wellness program can assist. A health and wellness component incorporated into an organizational adoption methodology can increase the pace, acceptance, and robustness of change in the organization. Consider the following questions:

- Are the attitudes and behaviors in your organization reflective of its core values?
- Do employees clearly understand and subscribe to the strategic direction of the organization?
- Are you experiencing increased productivity?
- Is employee morale high?
- Are changes implemented efficiently and effectively?

---

[3] http://www.adoptitsm.com/

If the answer to any of these question is no, then it is time to evaluate the effectiveness of how your organization manages changes and, in fact, embeds the change into the organizational DNA. Successful implementation of change affects customer satisfaction, employee engagement, organizational success, and, ultimately, the bottom line.

Often, a lack of success in projects, plans, and health and wellness initiatives is caused by a failure to effectively plan for the change, a failure to effectively manage the team, and/or failure to manage the implementation. Effective organizational change management involves employees in the process, clearly defines expected outcomes and behaviors, and results in a motivated leadership team with a workforce moving purposefully towards common goals. The failure to effectively implement changes manifests in many different forms with the commonality of negatively impact the bottom line.

An effective organizational adoption strategy that incorporates health and wellness as a keystone will demonstrate positive impetus towards successful implementation of changes regardless of whether you are implementing a small software upgrade or restructuring the entire organization.

We have found that when the organizational change includes direct benefits to employees, they are more likely to embrace it; when employees feel better, they are absent less, more productive, and more effective; and when employees are involved and they see their impact on an element of an organizational change, they feel empowered to positively impact the corporation's bottom line. Organizational change and health and wellness can be linked to increase the likelihood of success:

- A health and wellness program that follows an organizational change methodology for implementation will help to ensure the adoption and success of the program.

  An organizational change strategy that incorporates employee identified health and wellness components demonstrates to employees that the company is, in fact, committed to their wellbeing and recognizes the value they bring to the organization.

  Research has shown that when employees feel as though their company and leadership are committed to their wellbeing, they are more committed to the success of the organization.

- When healthy practices, such as healthy meetings, work life balance, stress reduction opportunities, and building community, are incorporated into the organizational change plan, the changes are more likely to be understood and effective.

  Even when changes are disruptive and difficult to implement, if employees recognize the benefits and feel that the company cares through a demonstrable focus on their health and wellness, they will be more likely to embrace the change.

Are you in the midst of change? Try the following to see the impact of incremental steps towards effective change adoption:

- **Listen** – What are the things that are impacting employee morale? Are there quick steps that you could take to address some of the underlying causes?

- **Communicate** – Have you clearly articulated the value proposition of the impending change? Not just what it means for the organization and its customers but also how it impacts the individual employees and teams.

- **Look at the overall change and identify three options for improving employee health and wellness as a part of the change.** If it is a physical move, what can be done in the new location to enhance employee health? Is there an opportunity for a walking trail or a meditation room? If it is a software rollout, perhaps provide training in a stress management technique, such as HeartMath™ prior to offering training. If it is an organization wide restructuring, it is a great opportunity to solicit employee input on ways to enhance work life balance.

- **Be leaders.** Model the behavior that you want to see in employees. This includes embracing organizational changes and adopting healthy behaviors.

Chapter 5: Healthy Project Management

What's a project manager to do? I spend time thinking about how to reconcile my vision of a healthy organization with the demands of project management for the project manager, for the project team, and for the bottom line of the organization. This is not an article about how to follow project management principles, there are great resources out there that talk about that and offer great value. Rather, I am focusing on the research based findings that integrating wellbeing into project management results in better outcomes.

As a facilitator, a consultant and a director in an operational setting, I have spent countless hours in conversations about why projects fail, root cause analyses, and lessons learned. As an analyst from a project management office I held people accountable to standards of practice. Nonetheless, projects continue to fail at often alarming rates and at great expense with the same explanations offered. We are not getting to the actual root cause and not correctly identifying the lessons. One critical missing piece is often organizational and individual wellbeing.

A healthy organization recognizes that integrating employee wellbeing into the project plan, the project itself, and the implementation plan is a key to success. Healthy employees in a healthy environment produce more effective, efficient, and successful project implementations. Research and science point to wellbeing as a key factor for an effective workplace. Where once it was a badge of honor to be found at work at 3AM or to walk in with dark rimmed circles under the eyes from a late night at the office, now science recognizes that we perform better and more efficiently when we have had eight hours of sleep.

Ten tips to incorporate into your project management to ramp it up to the next level

- **Plan realistically.** One of the best pieces advice I got as a project manager was to estimate a project as if someone else was doing it. In thinking about this, consider the individual's wellbeing and be realistic.

- **Lead a healthy lifestyle.** As a project manager, if you are not aware of and responsive to your personal wellbeing, you will not be able to be effective and, you will likely get sick or lose momentum for the project.

- **Be a healthy leader.** Team members take cues from the things that you do, rather than the things that you say. If they see you taking smoking breaks, they will join you. If they see you taking walks in the middle of the day, they will likely join you on that as well. Part of being a healthy leader is being able to communicate up the chain about your strategy and to demonstrate the successes that result. This is rarely easy. Being a part of the change that is needed in an organization you can be successful in your projects and recognized for the value of your message.

- **Sleep.** We now know that our bodies function better on eight hours of sleep a night. We also know that it is important to shut down computers, phones and other electronic devices a couple of hours before going to sleep. It is optimal to keep these devices out of the bedroom. As a project manager, this means considering realistically how much time a team member will have in a given week to work on a project. It means that when crunch time comes, it is often important to send people home or not look for answers to questions about the project at 11:00 PM. This is a significant adjustment for many organizations, but the truth is those late night answers are rarely useful and can be harmful.

- **Step away from the computer.** The Human Performance Institute talks about work not as a marathon but as a series of sprints. They recommend some sort of stretch or physical activity every 25-30 minutes. In fact, it is the recovery time from a work session where they say some of our best thinking is done. Try the Pomodoro Technique. Turn off email and distractions and work without interruption for 25 minutes. Then, take a five minute break, especially one that incorporates stretching or some exercise, followed by another

25 minute session. It is amazing how much you can accomplish and how much can get done.

- **Walk for your meetings.** Again science is our friend here. We now know that walking sparks creativity, that sitting all day is bad for us, that a break from the computer is good for us, and that walking every day is good for our health. Combine this and conduct walking meetings. If necessary, the agenda can be tracked and outcomes recorded on a SmartPhone.

- **Set reasonable deadlines.** When I went to the Center for Creative Leadership, we were assigned a project and the deadline kept being moved forward. This is reality for many of us. And, wanting to be appreciated, successful, or keep our jobs, we find a way to meet the deadline, to be "team players." In fact, though, we are often doing a disservice to the organization and ourselves. What if, instead, we provided a reasonable timeframe and when asked to adjust it, explained the impact. I'm a big fan of saying "yes, if" rather than "no, because." I think we can change a great deal with just those two words. "Yes, I can meet that revised deadline, if we remove an element of the deliverable, or if I can get assistance in a different area, or if I could skip these four meetings."

- **Build community.** I was on a project team once where they referred to us as the "dream team." We were, I must say, a group of very talented, well-seasoned consultants with broad and complementary experience. Little effort was expended to create community either within our team or between our team and our clients. As a result we never forged the types of bonds that would have enhanced our success. By taking the time to create a community on this team, our efforts would have been enhanced and some of our challenges avoided. There are many effective ways to build a community -- in the way the team is treated all of the time, in specific team building activities, and in joining together as a team to do something for others, perhaps a volunteer activity.

- **Manage stress.** According to WebMD, stress costs American industry more than $3 Billion annually. When we are stressed we make poor decisions, remember less, communicate poorly, and get sick. Working with a project team to manage stress, will improve results. There are many stress management tools available. I am a HeartMath® mentor and have found it to be a powerful tool for improving workplace efficiency.

- **Be Kind.** Science has shown us that our brains react better when we are kind to others and when we experience acts of kindness. All too often, for many of the reasons listed above, people choose not to be kind in the workplace and some even consider it a weakness. This tears apart the fabric of the team and will result in suboptimal outcomes.

- **And a bonus tip.** If nothing else, drink water and make healthy food choices. If you are providing snacks for your team - have whole fruits and vegetables available. You will be amazed at the difference just that will make. If you are dubious, try my sugar challenge[4]. You will feel better.

Most of these tips do not require additional work, they require working differently. By integrating them into project management, you will achieve considerable benefits. *It is simple and it works.*

---

[4] http://www.breakthroughconsultingllc.com/sugar-challenge.html

Be Strategic: Create a Healthy Organization

Healthy Leadership and Management

In Brief
Healthy practices lead to healthier results for the organization and the individual.

Ensure Effective Interactions
What We Know:
People can't keep up with the demands for interaction (email, meetings, etc)
The Old Way:
Conduct long meetings, send emails at all hours of the day
The Healthy Way:
- Conduct effective meetings
- Establish an email policy
- Communicate effectively
- Take breaks
- Be purposeful

Plan and Estimate Realistically
What We Know:
Plans often don't consider human factors
The Old Way:
Create a plan, assume it will work and then just work harder; time at the computer equals productivity
The Healthy Way:
- Establish a plan based on realistic estimates
- Recognize that people cannot be effective without adequate time away from the computer, sleep, exercise, etc.
- Think of work as a series of sprints with recovery time, not a marathon

STEP 1 Be a Healthy Leader
What We Know:
Eating well, exercising, reducing stress, and getting enough sleep lead to better outcomes
The Old Way:
Eat pizza, drink soda, work non-stop
The Healthy Way:
- Get enough sleep
- Eat healthy food, drink water
- Step away from the computer
- Exercise

STEP 3 Maintain a Healthy Work Environment
What We Know:
Standing and stretching are good for you; ergonomics matter
The Old Way:
Sit at your computer or in a meeting until the work is done
The Healthy Way:
- Take breaks, step outside, stretch, walk
- Create healthy ergonomics
- Consider plants in the workplace, use non-toxic products
- Don't conduct business at the bar or over cigarette breaks

Be Kind, Be Grateful
What We Know:
Kindness and gratitude in the workplace make a difference
The Old Way:
No time or need for kindness; yelling and brusqueness show strength
The Healthy Way:
- Listen, show empathy, be kind
- Smile
- Be honest
- Demonstrate and reward resilience

www.BreakThroughConsultingLLC.com
wendy@BreakThroughConsultingLLC.com

Wendy Kuhn

Chapter 6: Healthy Communication

Even when everything else is completely right, communicating poorly can tank a project, harm an organization, and lead to expensive mistakes or hours of re-work. Following some simple steps and strategies whether communicating one on one or in meetings and in person or via email, phone or texting can make an enormous difference in enhancing an organization's bottom line while also increasing employee wellbeing.

Communicate Well - Five Tips for Healthy Communication

It is valuable to pay attention to communication styles and, specifically, how to communicate in a healthier manner. We are assaulted with communication in many different forms and formats and expected to absorb information at an increasingly high rate and, often, while distracted. Here are five tips for healthy communication:

- **Use a common language.** When talking to or texting with someone, pay attention to how much they know about the subject matter. It is very easy, especially in business, to misinterpret an acronym or a technical word, leading a conversation down a rabbit hole, or worse creating costly mistakes and misunderstandings.

- **Listen with respect**. Often we assume we understand the other person's point of view, knowledge, or perspective or anticipate what they are going to say. As a result we half listen, misinterpret, or cut them off. This can lead to misunderstandings and mistakes as well as damage to relationships. Listening non-judgmentally with full attention and repeating back the essence, when appropriate, can be a huge step forward in these communications.

- **Step away.** When we are angry, stressed or frustrated, Cortisol courses through our systems making it really difficult to respond appropriately (and that Cortisol stays in our systems for hours after the stressful or frustrating event happened). Recognize when you are feeling a sub-optimal emotion and step away from the conversation. Even a few deep cleansing breaths can help you better respond.

- **Pay attention to body language.** If you are indicating disinterest by your body language, your eyes darting to the screen in front of you, or your attention clearly shifting to a different conversation, you are not going to have an effective, successful communication with the person in front of you regardless of what you or they say. If it is necessary to respond to a text or to answer a phone call, apologize and explain that you need to do so rather than trying to multi task, which few of can do and which conveys a message of disrespect or disinterest.

- **Practice healthy meetings.** In meetings, take frequent breaks and have people stretch at a moment when everyone is stuck. Define decision points and action items, start and end meetings on time, and provide water and healthy snacks. Have a clearly articulated agenda going into a meeting and identify action items and next steps at the end of the meeting with a follow up email if appropriate.

- **Accept that communication is hard and we all make mistakes.** If you or someone else has a communication flub or mishap, perhaps accept that we are all just doing the best we can, graciously acknowledge the mistake or accept an apology, and move forward with no lingering bad feelings.

Listen closely, validate what you think you heard, and respond appropriately. If your initial reaction is driven by anger, fear or stress, check in with yourself before responding. Be quick to forgive or to ask forgiveness when conversations take a bad turn. We sometimes mistake accessibility for urgency, just because we can respond immediately, it does not mean that we have to.

A deep cleansing breath, a moment of reflection, and a genuine connection to the other person can go a long way towards improved communication and increased efficiency in the work place.

Communicate Well by Leading Healthy Meetings

Often when thinking about Health and Wellness, organizations create a committee, initiate a program, or provide offerings through their insurance companies. All of these are valuable and relevant. In addition, it is important to incorporate health and wellness into the fabric of the organization's culture and to recognize that health and wellness includes not just fitness and eating well, but stress reduction, work life balance, volunteering, being a community, and having a sense of purpose.

As a corporate and government executive, I spent untold hours in meetings. All too often they started and ended late, there was little or no agenda, there were few accomplishments and I felt like I never had time to do my "real" work, which often led to frenetic lunches – eating with one hand while typing with the other or late evenings or early mornings. I believe that there is a better way. Through creating healthy meetings, an organization can take a giant leap towards a healthier, more productive work environment.

Healthy meetings are an easy and inexpensive way to begin to develop or expand an organizational culture that features employees who thrive, increase their productivity, and enhance the organization's bottom line.

A healthy meeting:

- **Has an agenda**. Distribute the agenda in advance, it can be attached to the calendar invite.

- **Is purposeful**. Provide a clear statement of the purpose at the beginning and a revisit at the end. There should be a measurable objective associated with the purpose that can be used to assess whether the conversation has gone off track and requires adjustment. If there is no clear purpose to the meeting, perhaps it does not need to occur.

- **Starts and ends at the scheduled time.** Schedule meetings to start five or ten minutes after the hour and/or end five or ten minutes before the hour. This provides participants time to stretch, check email, and complete work assignments between meetings. While this may feel as if meetings are being shortened, in fact, it should lead to meetings starting and ending on time (as people are not rushing from the previous meetings) and being more productive. Some companies actually track the cost of employee time lost due to meetings starting late and find that it is a significant cost.

- **Includes Water and Healthy Snacks**. Even when food or beverages are not served at the meeting, as a participant or leader model healthy behaviors, people will follow this lead.

- **Offers glasses and mugs for beverages.** Provide glass and mugs, rather than paper, plastic and Styrofoam, as they are both healthier and better for the environment.

- **Is conducted during a walk.** Consider, if it is only a two or three person meeting, having a walking meeting. Not only will you get some exercise and fresh air, but studies show that walking increases creativity.

- **Includes a stretch break.** Especially for long meetings, consider a stretching break. Sitting for long periods of time is demonstrated to be unhealthy. After stretching, people will return to their seats refreshed and with new ideas. There is research demonstrating that raising one arm at a time and stretching it backward and then forward increases creativity and improves solutions developed during meetings. Additionally, according to Amy Cuddy,[5] if the stretch break includes a two-minute power stretch, arms up over your head, people will feel more empowered and authentic when they return to their seats. Cuddy's research indicated that people who do a two minute power posture before job interviews are more likely to get the job – imagine harnessing that power in meetings!

---

[5]http://www.ted.com/talks/amy_cuddy_your_body_language_shapes_who_you_are?language=en

- **Allows participants to reduce stress.** If your team knows HeartMath® take a moment to reduce stress with this or another stress management technique at the beginning or during the meeting, especially if progress seems to be mired or things get tense or stressful. Conclusions reached during stressful meetings are often unworkable, have to be reconsidered, are not generally understood, or are not adopted.

- **Enables effective communication and active listening.** If the purpose of the meeting is to solicit input from participants (as compared to a meeting where information is being presented), ensure that you have accurately understood feedback and that anyone who wishes to speak is given the opportunity to do so.

- **Considers the location.** Don't require people to drink alcohol or smoke to be able to conduct business or have meetings. Having informal meetings in a social location is often a great choice, but be thoughtful about the location and employee the time of the meeting.

It is not easy to make the healthy choice the easy choice at work. While there is demonstrable evidence that reducing stress and improving health and wellness is good for a company's bottom line, if it is not incorporated into the routine aspects of conducting the business of the day, it is hard for it to be successful.

Conducting healthier meetings is one easy way for an organization to begin to experience the benefits of a healthier, more motivated and more engaged workforce.

Communicating Well by Making Email Work For You (and not Against You)

When I talk to people about work life balance and strategies to manage their energy to achieve their goals, the subject of email inevitably arises. It creates stress and pressure, it interferes with other work, and often interferes with non-work activities. It is also a key element for work productivity.

According to the Radicati Group, more than "100 billion emails are sent and received per day. Email is the predominant form of communication in the business space. This trend is expected to continue, and business email will account for over 132 billion emails sent and received per day by the end of 2017."

To be effective at work, it is often necessary to respond quickly to emails. At the same time, a response to one email then generates many more – like a multi-headed hydra where one head is cut off and two more appear. In addition, many people manage their personal lives, especially at work, through email.

There are a number of tools and strategies available to reduce your email load. Just because emails are delivered instantaneously, does not mean that we need to respond instantaneously, especially when involved in another task whether it is a conversation or driving. Within your workplace or among your team, agree to a set of email policies (perhaps based on the tips below) and then follow then. That way expectations will be appropriately set and email will work for you rather than against you.

- **Roll with it**. There are tools that will roll up and let you unsubscribe from lists that you are on. This way you can look at your subscriptions at your leisure rather than sorting through them and possibly missing emails that are actually directed to you. I use unroll.me

- **Schedule it**. While not possible for all people in all jobs, set specific blocks of time to read and respond to emails. Setting an alert for urgent emails (for example from your boss) might make this easier.

- **Don't go to bed with it**. Don't check emails after a certain time at night or before a certain time in the morning There is scientific evidence that time spent on a computer screen in the two hours before bed significantly interferes with sleep. Poor or insufficient sleep directly impacts job performance.

- **Read it**. Be sure to read the entire email. Especially on mobile devices, it is possible to miss part of an email if you don't scroll all the way down. While you may feel good about being able to quickly respond to an email, missing a key part, could lead to a huge email exchange and both a time and energy drain.

- **Use your phone to talk to people** Responding to important emails from a smart phone, unless absolutely necessary, often leads to miscommunication. Most of the time, for important issues, it is better to have a moment to think about it rather than responding on the run and responding on a larger device is easier and will enable you to be more thoughtful.

- **Do not require a reply.** Compose your email so that it does not require a reply. Often even something as simple as scheduling lunch, whether for business or pleasure, can require a 20 email exchange. "Where do you want to meet?", "I don't know, what do you think?", "I can do 11:30 but would you prefer 12:00?" Instead try short declarative sentences. "I'll meet you at Whole Foods for lunch at 11:45 in front of the salad bar unless I hear from you otherwise." You can even take it a step further as a friend of mine does and say "No Response Necessary" or "NRN."

- **No affect allowed.** Remember that email does not convey affect. If you are in the midst of a frustrating email conversation, consider that the other person or people might be equally frustrated. Pick up the phone and call or walk down the hall.

- **Copying is not always best.** Be thoughtful about who you copy (and especially who you bcc – in fact, I recommend never using bcc unless it is to hide the membership of a large distribution list.) Unnecessary copying will only increase your email volume.

- **Organize your email.** Create a structure that works for you and use it. Strive to handle each email only once, after you have read it file or label it appropriately so you don't need to revisit it.

- **It's a record.** Remember that you are creating a written record (especially if you work in a public records organization) and that you never know who might see your email. Reread it before you hit send, make sure it is something you want to say not just to the person to whom it is directed, but consider what other people might think if they see it. This actually applies to all social media.

- **B-r-e-a-t-h-e.** On important emails take a deep breath before hitting send, be sure it is what you want to say and how you want to say it. Consider that the recipient will not be able to see your face or hear your voice. Similarly, if you read an email that is distressing to you, take a moment to breathe and re-read it. Does it really say what you think it says, is it possible you are reading too much or too little into it? While it might feel like this requires time that is not available, an extra twenty or thirty seconds up front may save not only time down the road, but also anxiety and stress as well as money, clients, productivity, or revenue.

- **Text wisely.** Texting could probably be a category on its own, but perhaps I am old school enough to include it here. All of these same ideas apply to texting as well, but more so. Don't text and drive, or text and walk, or text and bike. Just don't do it. Few things are that urgent. Texting has replaced casual conversation. It is important to remember that it has no affect and its casual nature may lead to unnecessary misunderstandings. As with emails, it is hard to type long messages on a phone. It is easy to get out of synch where a text response is composed and sent while a different text comes in – leading to a very disjointed conversation. If a conversation is getting twisted, consider calling the person directly or switch to email.

- **Don't hit send when you are angry.** Anger clouds judgment. Even if anger is justified, an angry response will often exacerbate the problem and reflect poorly on the sender. Wait until the anger subsides, and then you will find it easier to articulate a more strategic, thoughtful, and effective response. Another choice is to write the email but not send it until you have a chance to review it the next morning. *It is astonishing how simple changes to email practices can save time, reduce stress, and increase efficiency and productivity.*

Chapter 7: Resilience at Work

When I was a consultant for a big consulting firm in Washington DC in the 90s, the definition of resilience at work was very clear: work long hours, bill many hours, eat a lot of pizza, drink heavily, overcommit, never ask for help, and never show or admit weakness.

I have been thinking a lot lately about what resilience at works looks like now, 25 years later. It is a fascinating time as we see three significant leaders stepping down over scandals in their organizations. These are people who a month ago probably would have fit a traditional business definition of resilience. The former CEO of Volkswagen, for example, worked his way to the top position and was recognized by Forbes as #58 on their list of powerful people last year. His name is now inextricably linked with cheating.

It is time to clarify what resilience means and look at how we can foster it in the workplace. There are two definitions that are important:

- The dictionary definition:
  "The ability to bounce back from adversity; the ability to become strong, healthy or successful again after something bad happens."

- Dr. Michael Ungar's (The Resilience Research Center in Canada[6]) definition:

    "*In the context of exposure to significant adversity, resilience is both the capacity of individuals to navigate their way to the psychological, social, cultural, and physical resources that sustain their well-being, and their capacity individually and collectively to negotiate for these resources to be provided in culturally meaningful ways.*"

What this says to me is that being resilient includes asking for and receiving help. Moreover, it does not require that people be treated poorly or that their wellbeing be ignored. In fact, it is just the opposite. Treating people disrespectfully and denying physical and emotional health undermine resilience.

There is no doubt that, regardless of how much advance planning we do, things go wrong in the workplace, and we will need resiliency. If they do not go wrong, we should question whether we are setting our sights too low. Projects fail, customers become unhappy, deadlines are missed, people get sick, etc. Sometimes these events are within our control and sometimes not. It is what happens after the event happens that fosters resilience and can lead to individual, group, and organizational success.

---

[6] http://resilienceresearch.org/

The way to build resilience in the workplace is inconsistent with the culture described above and inconsistent with the general activities of many organizations and individuals. Think about how often a negative event occurs and it is the fallout from the finger pointing, attempt to avoid being blamed, and cover up that cause the biggest problems. Key factors that interfere with resilience include:

- Lack of sleep.
- Time wasted blaming others or ourselves.
- Unnecessary heroics.
- Histrionics.
- Belief that the company or one's direct supervisor is not concerned about your wellbeing.
- Lack of collaboration and mutual support.
- Demeaning your own or others' sense of self-worth.
- Endless hours spent hunched over a computer without interruption.
- Abusive post mortems (I think the name says it all) focused on identify who to blame or how to avoid blame.

Instead, to foster resilience in the workplace:

1. Demonstrate resilient practices through healthy behaviors such as getting adequate sleep (this might mean not sending that 2 AM email), stepping away from the computer,

conducting productive meetings, exercising, and eating well and mindfully.
2. Create an environment where it is acceptable to ask for help and where people are rewarded for asking for help and for helping others.
3. Set realistic timeframes and goals and adjust them if necessary rather than looking to find someone to blame.
4. Be kind to others and express gratitude and appreciation.
5. Problem solve rather than blame.
6. Collaborate and look for ways to support others.

These steps alone will create a more resilient more effective workforce and will lead to fewer mistakes and improved outcomes.

Build Resilience by Using your Time Well - 9 Tips for Reducing The Busy Burden

My former husband used to complain that I had more free time than he did. I resisted the urge to point out that he had the exact same 24 hours per day as I did. It is true, though, that many of us feel that we are too busy and have too much to do while others, with the same amount on their plate, always seem to have available time.

Did you know that:

- Well educated American women have less leisure time than they did in 1965 and nearly 11 hours less per week than women who did not graduate from high school.
- Men with a college degree saw their leisure time drop by six hours between 1985 and 2005.
- 60% of those who use smartphones are connected to work for 13.5 hours or more a day.

We are distracted:

- It is estimated that we lose as much as 40% of our productivity when we try to multi-task.
- Cell phones are involved in 1.6 million auto crashes each year that cause a half million injuries and take 6,000 lives.

And we are not getting enough sleep:

- Chernobyl, Three Mile Island, the Exxon Valdez, and the explosion of the Challenger have all been partially attributed to sleep deprivation as well as more than 100,000 police reported automobile crashes each year.
- Medical residents, flight crews, and long distance truck drivers all have more requirements around how long their shifts can be and how much down time there is between shifts than there used to be.

This led me to think about steps we can take to reduce our busy burden, especially at work. Here are some of my conclusions:

- **Keep your heart and your head where your feet are (most of the time).** By staying present and engaged during the workday, we are less likely to make mistakes that require rework or to engage in miscommunications that can be costly in terms of time and money. When you need a mini-break, step away from the computer or work and meditate, stretch, enjoy looking at pictures of your family, or schedule that next vacation, imagining how soft the sand will feel underfoot. Then return fully present to the task at hand.

- **Sleep**. When we operate with insufficient sleep, we are inefficient and ineffective. Moreover, we are more likely to make sub-optimal decisions and have accidents. Try to get seven to eight hours of sleep each night.

- **Step away from the device.** Spending more time on our electronic devices does not lead to increased productivity. A break from them does. During the workday, take frequent five minute breaks, especially when you feel you can least afford it. At home, have device free rooms or times to fully engage your head and your heart where your feet are. Step away from your devices a couple of hours before going to sleep, to increase your likelihood of having a good night's sleep. And consider exercise, it's great for your body, your health, your mind, and your heart.

- **Be comfortable.** During the workday, good ergonomics matter. If you are uncomfortable, it is difficult to fully engage and the added stress on your body of the discomfort will show itself in sub-optimal performance. Take stretch breaks during meetings, wear shoes that allow you to participate in walking meetings, have an appropriate computer setup, and wear clothes that are comfortable.

- **Be grateful and be kind.** Expressing gratitude and kindness to others will likely result in a team effort with work getting done more quickly and efficiently. Kindness and gratitude are also good for your brain, in fact, a feeling of gratitude will increase productivity. Even if you don't have the opportunity to express gratitude, take a moment to feel it or write it down.

- **Smile.** When we smile at people and they smile back, they are more likely to be receptive to our request or conversation. It also improves our own mood.

- **Conduct healthy meetings.** All too often meetings are poorly run, resulting in excessive time spent in the meetings and insufficiently defined or understood outcomes. Schedule meetings to start five minutes after the hour, enabling people to arrive on time from their previous meeting. Follow an agenda with a clearly stated purpose. End the meeting when it is over with clearly stated action items and decisions. If it is a long meeting, take stretch breaks and provide healthy snacks. If it is a small group meeting, consider a walking meeting.

- **Be intentional.** Often people are busy because they do not focus with clear intentions on the intended outcome or plan. Be focused. Whether it is a business activity or a personal conversation, give others the gift of your complete attention and be clear of your own desired outcomes.

- **Decompress.** Often the time in the car or on the subway is seen as lost or wasted time. Consider instead that it is an opportunity to decompress and transition from work to home. This of course means not picking up work again upon arriving at home. Find techniques that work for you during your driving or commuting times that help you make that mindset shift. Exercising on the way to or from work can also be a great practice for decompressing.

There is no question that there are many conflicting demands on many of us and many people's lives are tightly scheduled or often feel overwhelming.

Pick simple steps that can help ease the feeling of overwhelm and you will soon benefit from the increased resilience this brings to you.

Chapter 8: Be Happy at Work

We all work in a wide variety of office environments – for some people, like me, our office is also our living room couch, for others it's a cubicle or an office, for others, it's an airplane and a hotel room.

For all of us, regardless of where we work or for whom we work, there are ways to make the work day healthier and happier.

Here are some suggestions.

1. **Breathe.** Find multiple times in your day to take a deep, calming breath. I used to take the time when I was waiting for my laptop to load or reboot to take deep cleansing breaths.
2. **Eat in while eating out.** Bring your own lunch whenever you can. You will save money and probably eat healthier. However, still use lunch as an opportunity to step away from your desk maybe eat outside somewhere, at a break room, or share a meal with a friend.
3. **Eat mindfully.** Even if it's for only a few minutes, take the time to focus on your meal, be grateful for the nourishment it is providing to you, and enjoy it
4. **Take the stairs, whenever you can.** My pet peeve is when I see a sign in a building suggesting that I take the stairs, but

the sign is on the elevator door – by that time I've already pushed the button and, often, I have no idea where the stairs are. Celebrate that you know where the stairs are hidden and take them!

5. **Take a walk, every day, wherever you are**. Get outside if possible and consider a walking meeting. A walk will actually increase creativity.
6. **Move**. Create an office space that is ergonomically comfortable and that requires that you stand up or move frequently to complete routine tasks.
7. **Drink water.** Water is good for you, not only will you stay hydrated and avoid drinking calorie and chemically laden beverages, but it will force you to get up throughout the day.
8. **Stretch every twenty minutes**. Take a pause in what you are doing and stretch some part of your body. Stand up and stretch if you can. Stretch your neck, your arms, or your legs and use that moment to take a quick mental break, assess how you are feeling, any needs you might have, and **b-r-e-a-t-h-e**!
9. **Feel Gratitude.** Take a moment during the workday to be grateful for the gifts in your life. ***Gratitude helps your brain!***

Be Happy - Just Say Yes

I was at a women's networking event recently where the speaker encouraged people to "Just say no" – no to taking on new commitments, to doing things we didn't want to do, or just for the practice of saying no. No, she told us, is a complete sentence   I felt like a fish out of water. While I accept that many of us do too much for all sorts of reasons, I am not convinced that we should spend so much energy celebrating putting "no" out into the universe.

What if, instead, we said "yes"?

- Yes, I can help you with that if you can help me figure out childcare.
- Yes, I would love to take on a new project, can we figure out together how to solve my concern about having time to get it done?
- Yes, I would love to come visit you, I'm worried about traffic, I'll come next weekend.
- Yes, I will make time in my life for you because I know that what matters in life is the people and the connections, not the work.
- Yes, I want to listen to you, truly deeply listen, can we find a time when I am not preoccupied with other things?
- Yes, I care about you.

Clearly, sometimes we need to say no, but I do not think it should be our default. I do not think it is necessarily a sign of strength, independence, or courage, even though sometimes it can be. I think yes can be a sign of strength, independence and courage as well.

What if there is something to Karma and to what you put out in the universe? To me, it seems better to state the positive rather than the negative. In self-hypnosis, they teach that your unconscious can't actually process the negative, so it is necessary to create a positive intention. "I will sleep better" rather than "I won't have trouble falling asleep." Think about how hard it is to not think about elephants once you have said to yourself "don't think about elephants." It is so much easier, instead, to just think about giraffes – do that and the elephant is nowhere in sight.

The networking session I mentioned particularly troubled me because it was full of young women, building their careers.

We who are "of a certain age" have so much wisdom and experience to offer – is the best we can do to say "No." Please, instead, can we say, "Yes and here's how?"

Be Happy.. Be Kind in the Workplace

When I was a teenager (a long time ago), I had a temp job that made a big impression on me. Every morning I would come in and sit at the typewriter (yes, actual typewriter) and do whatever tasks had been assigned to me. Grim looking people hustled around doing serious appearing tasks. Then, one morning, I came in and a group of people were laughing and telling jokes in the hallway for two or three minutes before beginning their day's work. It turned out that the boss was coming in late that morning. My supervisor told me that those few minutes of laughter made the day go better with smoother interactions and increased productivity, but the boss had neither patience nor tolerance for those brief, positive interactions. I have since worked in a number of environments with bosses who were unkind, who saw yelling as an acceptable management style, or who saw my kindness as a weakness. It makes no sense to me. I have always believed that being kind in the workplace is an asset, not a liability.

How validating to learn from Dr. David Hamilton[7] that being kind is actually good for you and for those around you. Being kind can improve confidence, control, happiness, and optimism. It leads to positive physiological changes in the brain, decreases isolation and increases connectedness. It is good for our actual, physical hearts. Maybe when we say "you did my heart good", we mean it more

---

[7] http://drdavidhamilton.com/the-5-side-effects-of-kindness/

literally than we realize. It actually does not matter if people reciprocate kindnesses, it is the act itself that is beneficial (not to mention all of the Karmic benefits). On top of the benefits for ourselves when we are kind, Dr. Hamilton's research also shows that when people observe others being kind, they are more likely to be kind.

With all of the benefits of kindness, I started to think about easy acts of kindness in the workplace. Here's my list:

- **Refill paper in the printer, start a fresh pot of coffee, or pick up something that's fallen over.** It will likely take less time to do it then it would take to ask someone else to do it. In my first job out of college, I acquired the skill of removing jammed paper from a copy machine. It has served me well over the years.

- **Smile and say hello to people in the hallway or people in the elevator, even strangers.** When I was in college we had a deep and serious exploration of issues on campus after a suicide shocked our small, liberal arts community. One of the takeaways was how impactful it could be for people to simply take the time to say hello to each other. A few years later, I applied this in a work environment where all of the first year employees took it as a personal challenge to make eye contact with and greet the more seasoned staff. A huge win was when the senior staff responded in kind.

- **Say "yes if" rather than "no because."** While there is a lot of pressure, especially on women, to learn how to say no, I think that it is sometimes more powerful to say "yes if." Perhaps, "yes, I can stay late and help you finish this report if you can proofread this letter for me that has to go out today." Or, "yes, I can meet with you if you can make it a walking meeting so I can get outside today and enjoy the beautiful fall weather." Or, "yes, I can meet with you, but I want to give you my full attention, so can we do it later this afternoon?"

- **Say please and thank you.** If something is praiseworthy, let others know. I have a friend who describes herself as a "please and thank you kind of girl" and so, even on Twitter, she always says thank you – "thanks for the retweet," "thanks for the mention," "thanks for the great article." And, the truth is, that causes me to retweet her more.

- **Be a kindness leader.** People model their behaviors on what they see in the workplace. Through modeling kindness, you create kindness and in doing so, create a healthier, more vibrant and more productive work environment.

Margaret Mead said, *"Never doubt that a small group of thoughtful, committed citizens can change the world; indeed, it's the only thing that ever has."* Maybe this applies to kindness in the workplace.

Maybe if we are kinder in the workplace, we will be kinder out of the workplace. And, just maybe, this will increase the level of kindness in the world.

Be Happy - Keep Your Head and Your Heart Where Your Feet Are

It seems to me that "busy" has become the standard response to the question of "how are you?" And, many of us are.

According to a new Pew Research Center study[8], four in ten full time working mothers always feel rushed. I can see my friends who are parents rolling their eyes, "ya think?"

For many of us, busy often means that we want to be in multiple places at one time. When we are home, we are distracted by emails coming in from work and when we are at work we are worried about a sick child, an aging parent, or the long list of errands still to be done. This is often amplified by being overtired from a poor or insufficient night's sleep.

I have been pondering whether alignment of our heads, hearts, and feet could help with the epidemic of busyness. When we have our heads, hearts and feet aligned:

- **We sleep**. Our bed is the place for sleep (and sex) and nothing else. Recognizing the need for 7-8 hours of sleep a night and taking steps to achieve that need reduces our busyness as we can be more effective in our waking

---

[8] http://www.pewsocialtrends.org/2015/11/04/raising-kids-and-running-a-household-how-working-parents-share-the-load/

hours. This increases our alignment, as we are not distracted by exhaustion.

- **We pay attention when we respond to others via email, phone, text or in person.** I have not found a good study that looks at lost time and dollars due to inattentive communications, but I have no doubt it is huge. A quick, thoughtless aside in a conversation, an email that inadvertently excludes the word "not", or a phone conversation with a distracted driver can be immensely expensive and emotionally painful. Being present in a conversation is not only more authentic, but is a significant reduction in the "busy" burden.

- **We are clear on our priorities.** To align our feet, head and heart, we often first have to ensure that our feet are in the right place for us for now. So often distraction, multi-tasking, and lack of focus occur when our feet are not where we want them to be.

There was a great line in the book "Cheaper by the Dozen." You might recall that the father was obsessed with creating time saving devices and was often asked what the point of saving all of that time was. His response was "for whatever you want."

Be mindful of how you use your time, we all have exactly 24 hours in a day (give or take). By aligning our heads, our hearts, and our feet, we can make that most of that time. Choose wisely, because one day we do, in fact, run out.

Be Happy Be Kind

"Be Kind Whenever Possible; It is always Possible"

Dalai Lama

On a recent trip to Dallas, I was delighted by the number of acts of kindness I experienced, whether it was on the running trail or as I was trying to cross an insanely busy street at the cross walk. I've been thinking a lot about kindness lately. While my Facebook feed is filled with memes of kindness, cute puppies, and old friends appearing to say hi, there is much in the world around us and in people's behaviors that is not kind. Perhaps the Facebook feed is a reflection of how desperately we are searching for kindness. I think being kind online is great, I am always happy to share posts about kindness and happiness, but I think actual, in person, human kindness trumps all. Some of my thoughts on kindness:

- **Be Grateful.** It is easier to be kind when you are experiencing a positive outlook and it turns out that being grateful can create a positive outlook. Try this: for thirty days write down three things for which you are grateful, as you are writing actually experience the feeling of gratitude. As you go about your day, see if you are feeling a little bit kinder to others.

- **Spend some time alone, in nature if possible.** Ironically, it might be that one of the best ways to be kind to others is to be sure to give yourself some time to be alone, perhaps it's about being kind to yourself so that you can be kind to others.

- **Give hugs freely.** I'm not necessarily recommending hugging strangers in the street (although that is an interesting social experiment), but hug the people close to you, sincerely, with intention and with affection. They and you both will experience that as kindness.

- **Recognize that sometimes being kind is more important than being right (and accept that you are unlikely to change my world view and vice versa).** It is interesting and informative to have debates about different points of view and different perspectives. It is not informative to be mean to each other or to express these views in cruelty. Accept that people see the world differently and even learn information differently. Healing the anger, hate and mistrust that seems to be appearing on the political and social stage daily is a huge undertaking and can begin with simple acts of kindness among friends and strangers.

- **Say please and thank you.** Perhaps it should go without saying, but following the basic manners we learned growing up can go a long way towards being kind and having people be kind to you. You don't have to agree with everything someone says or even like them very much, but there is actually no reason, not to be polite.

I teach a class on healthy project management in which I recommend that project managers create healthy policies for their team. I am often asked what policies around kindness would look like. What do you think? What does kindness look like at home and in the workplace? What would you add to my list above?

Chapter 9: Continue at Home

An approach to wellbeing in the workplace has to also consider wellbeing at home. Ultimately wellbeing is about incorporating practices into the fabric of our being regardless of where we are. Healthy practices translate into enhanced wellbeing.

Get enough sleep!

Increasingly, the evidence is that getting a solid night's sleep is beneficial for us in every way. Sleep helps our immune system, reduces stress, can help prevent weight gain, and generally puts us in a better mood. Some suggestions on how to get a good night's sleep:

- Remove your wireless electronics from your bedroom.
- Use your bed for sleeping, nighttime reading, and sex. Nothing else!
- If you find yourself waking up often in the middle of the night, it might be from hunger. Try eating a little bit of protein before going to bed.
- Give yourself some decompression time before going to bed -- turn off the TV, step away from the Internet, turn off the music.
- If you exercise in the evenings, be sure you finish at least three hours before going to bed and definitely exercise!
- Follow a similar nighttime ritual each night.

- Don't go to bed angry -- kiss your loved ones good night.

If you find that you are going through the day tired or falling asleep, or if you snore loudly, consider going to a medical professional to determine if something more is going on with you.

There is nothing more fabulous than getting out of bed in the morning fully energized to face the day, confident you can take on the world -- take the steps you can to make that happen!

Eat Mindfully

I believe that the process of eating is as important as the food that you eat -- well, maybe not quite as important, but very important nonetheless! By making sure that you eat your meals consciously and deliberately, you will feel better, you will experience your food more deeply (thus leading you to make healthier food choices), and you will be healthier. What does this look like?

- Chew each bite of food 20 or 30 times. Once you do that easily, try increasing it to 40 or 50 times. Your system will work more smoothly, you will find it easier to savor your food, and you will likely experience tastes you don't usually experience and enjoy.

- Watching Downton Abbey the other night, I noticed Lady Mary being called in to a formal meal on her own. Each meal does not need to be a formal state occasion, but take the time to set a place for yourself at a table. Make eating an enjoyable timeout from your otherwise busy, hectic life. A meal is a great opportunity to hit the pause button on your day. If you have a family, use it as a time to reconnect with them, focus your attention on the meal, and enjoy the whole experience.

- Breathe before you start. Take a moment before starting to eat to take a deep breath. Be fully present in the moment. Know that whatever else is going on with your day, this is a time to nourish yourself, mind, body and spirit.

- Think about your food as a life force. Find a way to send energy to the food and to thank it for nourishing you. If you find Reiki to be a practice you relate to, hold your hands over your meal for a moment and channel life energy, if you say a prayer before meals, do that.

These practices will make meal time more enjoyable and will nourish you in a way that mindlessly consuming food, even the healthiest food, in a car or in front of the TV will not.

Good, healthy, delicious, lovingly prepared food, shared with loved ones or eaten alone is one of the great gifts of our world -- Cherish it!

Increase your Energy

Do you feel tired frequently?

Lately, I have been part of a lot of conversations about energy. Many of us struggle with energy issues -- some folks have too much, some of us feel that we don't have enough. It's always useful to get a medical evaluation to find out if something is going on, in addition, I thought some quick tips for energy might be useful.

For example, if you sniff a lemon it can give you an energy boost, and improve your mood at the same time. Drinking water can also help to boost your energy. You can combine the two by adding a slice of fresh lemon to your water. Take a deep inhale of the lemon scent before dropping it into the water.

By the way, just to be clear, I am talking about the scent of an actual lemon, or, perhaps, a pure essential oil. I am not talking about an artificially created scent or fragrance!

Be Happy - Be Grateful

Our brains are wired to have a positive response to feelings of gratitude, leading us to want to experience it more. As we experience gratitude, our brains look for more things for which to be grateful. Because of the brain activity associated with feeling grateful, feelings of gratitude can lead us to exercise more, feel less stress, and even reduce our aches and pains.

One of the nice things about experiencing gratitude is that it does not require a huge amount of time or mental energy. You can experience gratitude when you express a heartfelt thank you to a friend or loved one, it can be encompassed in a hug, or it can be a fleeting appreciation of a beautiful hummingbird in a feeder.

I asked my Facebook friends how they show gratitude and for what they are grateful. Here are some of the things that I learned from them. My grateful friends:

- Shower their children with hugs and kisses
- Participate actively in the community
- Take good care of themselves
- Spend time with and care for their loved ones
- Enjoy their life.

For me, while I try to express gratitude throughout the course of a day, I tend to take the time when I am doing my morning pages to pause and focus on a gratitude list. The amazing Julia Cameron, in the book "The Artist's Way,"[9] talks about writing morning pages. First thing in the morning, while still in a semi-awake state, I plug in the coffee, let the dog out, and sit in the aforementioned porch, pen and journal in hand. Not all of the time but often, as I write, I make a list of the things that I appreciate. My husband is always at the top, followed closely by the poodle. Then the list can go in any number of different directions. Perennial favorites include my family, my friends, my health, and my coffee. In addition to all of the great brain activity I am apparently generating by doing this, I feel that it also brings me into the present moment, aware of what *is* at that point in time. And, I find that when I do this, my days are smoother, great things happen, and I feel happier.

Based on my experience and that of my friends, here are seven great ways to express gratitude. .

- Write morning pages
- Create an evening appreciation list
- Give extra hugs to loved ones
- Pay it forward with kindness
- Send a hand-written note to express gratitude

---

[9] http://juliacameronlive.com/

- Say thank you
- Pause and breathe in appreciation and breathe out gratitude.

Being grateful may make life run just a little smoother and be good for your brain as well!

Find Joy - Avoid Toxic People

I spend a lot of time thinking about (and writing about) avoiding toxins in our personal care and home cleaning products. But what about toxic people? Toxic energies? In my HeartMath® training, we learned about how the heart sends a magnetic field out from the body. The goal of HeartMath®, which is a stress reduction tool (and so much more), is achieving a state called coherence.

The magnetic field created by a state of coherence is so powerful that if you hang out with people who are in a state of coherence, just by being with them you will become coherent, your stress level will go down.

So, why not hang out with happy people, people who make you feel good, people who say, as Shel Silverstein did:

"Listen to the mustn'ts, child. Listen to the don'ts. Listen to the shouldn'ts, the impossibles, the won'ts. Listen to the never haves, then listen close to me... Anything can happen, child. Anything can be."

When you spend time with people who believe that anything is possible and encourage you to dream, how does that make you feel? Is that how you want to feel?

My years in IT and project management have taught me that it is important to think about the don'ts, to think about what could happen, to plan for contingencies, but the dreamer in me knows that to soar, to be awesome, to be me, I also have to believe that anything is possible.

Spending time with people who can help me soar is a joy.

Sometimes, even often, this means spending time with people who challenge my beliefs, who ask if something is truly possible, and that's great. Spending time with people who are toxic to me however is not great. Figuring out the difference between the two might be a lifelong journey.

Chapter 10: What's Next?

We live in tumultuous times. There is a great deal of talk about broad generational differences. As the Baby Boomers age, the millennials advance and settle into work life, and generation Xers are sandwiched in between the two; workplaces are struggling with difficult and complex problems as the generations seem to separate and work at odds with each other rather than in harmony with each other. I am convinced that an approach to the workplace that incorporates employee wellbeing into the fabric of their culture will have the added benefit

ABOUT THE AUTHOR

Wendy Kuhn is a strategic planning and implementation consultant, a HeartMath® Mentor, and a Health Coach. She brings more than twenty years of experience to her writing, coaching, and consulting. Wendy is committed to working with organizations to incorporate employee wellbeing into the fabric of their culture and with individuals to incorporate health and wellness into the fabric of their being. Learn more at www.BreakThroughConsultingLLC.com.

Wendy, her husband, Matt, and their twelve pound poodle live in Chapel Hill North Carolina.

www.ingramcontent.com/pod-product-compliance
Lightning Source LLC
Chambersburg PA
CBHW061443180526
45170CB00004B/1535